May
2017

The Re-Awakening:

A Workbook to Get Unstuck and Awaken to Your Life's Purpose

Toshia Shaw

Time 2 Shine

ISBN 978-0-9740426-7-1

This is a work of fiction. It is not meant to depict,
portray or represent any particular real persons. All
the characters, incidents, and dialogues are the
products of the author's imagination and are not to
be construed as real. Any references or similarities
to actual events, entities, real people, living or dead,
or to real locales are intended to give the novel a
sense of reality. Any similarity in other names,
characters, entities, places, and incidents is entirely
coincidental.

Editor – Write On Promotions
Purple Wings Publishing
3180 W. Sahara Ave., Suite C20
Las Vegas, NV 89102
www.purplewingsbooks.com

Table of Contents

Dedication
Introduction
Chapter 1   Identity Crisis: Who Am I & What Do I Want
Chapter 2   Owning Up to Yesterday: The Key to Shaping Today
Chapter 3   The Art of Surrendering, Acceptance and Forgiveness
Chapter 4   Change your Tape: Stopping the Negative Mind Chatter
Chapter 5   What Is Your Focus?
Chapter 6   The Law of Attraction: You Can Get What You Want!
Chapter 7   Decision Making
Chapter 8   Establishing Healthy Self-Esteem & Self-Respect
Chapter 9   Creating Boundaries for Healthy Relationships
Chapter 10   Cultivating Self-Care: (Check Up On It, and Check It Out)
Chapter 11   Connecting With the Divine
Chapter 12   Forget Fear
Chapter 13   The Importance of Authenticity & Living in Your Truth
Chapter 14   Moving Forward: Where Do You Go From Here?
About the Author
References

Dedication

*To all of the people who have trusted me and
allowed me to come into contact with their spirit
guide, I am grateful. You are truly the teacher, and
I have learned something from each one of you.
Thank you.*

Introduction

A few decades ago, the concept of life coaching was as strange as they come. By the way, why would anyone need a life coach? That was the prevalent mentality.

Today, life coaching has grown into a worldwide phenomenon and people in their dozens, are finally coming to that realization that they can benefit from the wisdom and experience of a life coach; in my case, a one-on-one mentor.

The degree to which both mentoring and life coaching have proven efficiency is linked, usually, to the life experience (and/formal training) on the part of the mentor; it is reminiscent of the experiences of the one who needs coaching/mentoring.

Take for example, myself- a trauma coach, an honor vested upon me by my battle with, and subsequently freedom from post-traumatic stress disorder. (A trauma life coach is an individual who has had formal training in the field of trauma, and post-traumatic stresses disorder (PTSD); or has experienced trauma/PTSD and successfully healed from it.)

When I finally got healed from my PTSD symptoms, my heart went out to those with similar experiences, those who were still stuck in their past, re-living and re-experiencing negative memories, and consequently, unable to lead normal lives. I wanted, so badly, to help!

Today, as a professional mentor to individuals worldwide, I have successfully compiled the key elements that have over time, helped my clientele not only recognize who they are and what they want out of their lives, but the key factors that kept them stuck, isolated, and incapable of enjoying their freedom and regardless of the traumatic specifics, they always had some things in common. These are adequately depicted by the topics contained herein.

By means of this workbook, I am glad to say that several of them were able to heal, launching forward with so much zeal, into the future of their dreams. It is with so much excitement that I report that the success rate of my clients who take my three-month professional mentorship, The Re-Awakening has been phenomenal.

Each person shed PTSD symptoms, recognized or devised a promise that they are now fulfilling in their lives, and surrendered to the spirit to achieve maximum freedom.

As I kept thinking about ways to help other post-traumatic individuals, it finally dawned on me that I wouldn't be able to, on a one-on-one basis, mentor every one of them. It was in recognition of the fact that everyone won't have the luxury of being mentored by me that I developed this workbook.

My main aim, my passion, is to help you get unstuck and awaken to your life's purpose.

Getting open and being 100% real is the way to go, even if it involves picking pieces of your shattered heart- that is, if you truly want to get unstuck.

Once you are able to achieve this, you will discover, sometimes painfully, how to heal and move forward. Be reminded that no matter how painful it seems, there is definitely light at the end of the tunnel! Keep an open mind and finally, do the work.

Love & Light,

Toshia
SHAW

"I feel keeping a promise to yourself is a direct reflection of the love you have for yourself. I used to make promises to myself and find them easy to break. Today, I love myself enough to not only make a promise to myself, but I love myself enough to keep that promise"

-Steve Maraboli, Life, the Truth, and Being Free

CHAPTER 1

IDENTITY CRISIS: WHO AM I & WHAT DO I WANT?

"Our morals, values, and emotional intelligence make up who we are at our core."

I am seated, suited and all this sunny afternoon, in my office. A new client is seated in front of me, and after the exchange of a few pleasantries, we get down to business. She looks at me, obviously interested in my next line of action.

I give a slight nod, followed by a question:

"Who are you?" This is one of the interesting parts of my job. I watch her go through a myriad of physical reactions, ranging from wringing of her hands, brow perspiring and deep sighs. Finally, she lays back in her chair, as she stares back at me in wide-eyed amazement. This is followed by a not so uncommon response to my question:

"Wow, that's a good question."

The Re-Awakening

I am not in the least, surprised. In actual fact, if she hadn't responded in this way, I may have tagged her atypical. In other words, most of my clientele have this same response to my seemingly benign question. It is a question not frequently asked, and to which most have no answer.

I expect these responses, because it's why I have been sought me out as a life-coach in the first place.

However, most of my clients do not know this. My question makes them very uncomfortable. This is why before I even begin to work with a person I tell them, "Get comfortable with being uncomfortable." Life-coaching on this level means I will have to strip them naked and make them stand in front of the mirror, a vivid description of self-reflection. Now of course, I do not strip them naked figuratively, but I do so mentally.

Why are we so unhappy? To what end do we feel mentally exhausted? Why do you feel stagnant? As a matter of fact, getting to the bottom of why we are unhappy, stagnant, mentally exhausted, etc., is serious work. We would rather make up a new persona than face our own issues, in other words, pretense is easier than reality. Heck, some of us have gotten so used to pretending, it has become our reality!

Because I have insight into this vital aspect of human living, I dare not take my work lightly. I have deep respect and honor for people who can say, enough is enough! I've had it living with the mask of happiness when deep down inside my body is wrought with pain.

I am full of empathy for people in this shoe because I was that girl! And each day, after suffering major sexual and violent trauma I put on my fitted mask. It had become so accustomed to my face that you probably couldn't make out one from the other. I had become a chronic liar, lying to myself that everything was fine.

After delicate painting of my face, I appeared indeed, to be a well-coifed lady, who had her shit together. Which was pretty hilarious, because when I was alone at night, I fell apart! Countless nights I cried myself to sleep.

Eventually, I got tired of living the lie, and not being able to figure out why I couldn't live the life God promised me. That was when I made The Pact. Out of desperation, I decided that I would do whatever was necessary to find out the true source of my mental anguish, eradicate it, find my purpose, get spiritually in tune with GOD, and get free. It wasn't easy! Oh my goodness, I fought myself along the way. The truth was much too painful to bear. I gave my clinical therapist a hard time. After my clinician did all he could for me, I sought out non-traditional treatment and the real work began. I started to uncover my truths, and little by little I found Toshia again.

I actually started to like her; allowing bits and pieces of her to be seen. Then eventually, the real Toshia came out and I've been soaring every since. I am now living fully in Dharma. To live in dharma is to live harmoniously in nature and in your destiny. There is a balance in which you live authentically. The balance of living the life you want while living harmoniously with what spirit wants.

If you are in any way like me, you would have asked, over and over again, questions such as 'Who am I?' the real challenge lies in giving an appropriate answer to this question. And to be able to do this, to find out who you truly are at your core, it's important to define your ethics, morals, and values. They are usually influenced and taught to us by our environment, parents, teachers, religion, etc.

That is, the rules you live by were set into place long before you were born. They are those rules that survived generations. We simply went along with it because it was how we were taught. It was what was expected of us and generally, we don't start to question these rules until we start to think for ourselves. At a particular age, which is individual-specific (there is no one-size-fits-all principle for this), we start to notice differences, are able to read these differences, or feel these differences inside of us. Then we begin to question how we were raised and we begin to set new rules which become our new ethics, morals, and values that we live by, and in turn teach others around us in our own environment.

Ethics are rules that help guide us and differentiate what is right and wrong. They are put into place to help us do the right thing. In businesses these are rules that have been set so that employees have a set of rules to go by to help that business structured in such a way that employees treat each other and customers in a good light.

Ethics are put into place to ensure each person has the same value regardless of their personal values (Hopefully I'm not losing you here.) For instance, say in an individual's personal life honesty isn't a value of theirs. So if the person doesn't value honesty, how would this fare if they worked at a bank? Not so good! Integrity is one of the most important ethics put into place at a bank. So while that person is working at that bank, they practice honesty because it is part of the ethics of that company.

Values are a personal view of what is important to you as an individual. They also help you make decisions between right and wrong. Your values are the things that you believe are important in the way that you live your life. They help you govern your priorities, they're possibly the processes you use to tell if things are going right or wrong within your life.

Values help you determine things like:
1. Is this what I really want to do my life?
2. Should I try this drug?
3. Do I really want to turn out like my parents?

Below I have a list of values, which will help you develop a clearer sense of what is most important to you in your life. Of course this list is not at all exhaustive, as there is an endless list of things in which people find most important in their lives. However, these are some of the things that my clients have come up with.

It would be best if you marked the values that are most important to you now, and then make a list of these values in order of priority. As you look over this list some values may have little to no significance; or they might even seem offensive to you! Just list the values that resonate within you now. Don't see some values on this list? Then add them to your own list.

Remember; only list those that are important to you now.

Abundance	Artistry
Acceptance	Assertiveness
Accessibility	Assurance
Accomplishment	Attentiveness
Accountability	Attractiveness
Accuracy	Audacity
Achievement	Availability
Acknowledgement	Awareness
Activeness	Awe
Adaptability	Balance
Adoration	Beauty
Adroitness	Being the best
Advancement	Belonging
Adventure	Benevolence
Affection	Bliss
Affluence	Boldness
Aggressiveness	Bravery
Agility	Brilliance
Alertness	Buoyancy
Altruism	Calmness
Amazement	Candor
Ambition	Care
Amusement	Capability
Anticipation	Carefulness
Appreciation	Camaraderie
Approachability	Certainty
Approval	Celebrity
Art	Challenge
Articulacy	Change

Charity
Charm
Chastity
Cheerfulness
Clarity
Cleanliness
Clear-mindedness
Cleverness
Closeness
Comfort
Commitment
Community
Compassion
Competence
Competition
Completion
Composure
Concentration
Confidence
Conformity
Congruency
Connection
Consciousness
Conservation
Consistency
Contentment
Continuity
Contribution
Control

Conviction
Conviviality
Coolness
Cooperation
Cordiality
Correctness
Country
Courage
Courtesy
Craftiness
Creativity
Credibility
Cunning
Curiosity
Daring
Decisiveness
Decorum
Deference
Delight
Dependability
Depth
Desire
Determination
Devotion
Devoutness
Dexterity
Dignity
Diligence
Direction

8

Directness	Excellence
Discipline	Excitement
Discovery	Exhilaration
Discretion	Expectancy
Diversity	Expediency
Dominance	Experience
Dreaming	Expertise
Drive	Exploration
Duty	Expressiveness
Dynamism	Extravagance
Eagerness	Extroversion
Ease	Exuberance
Economy	Fairness
Ecstasy	Faith
Education	Fame
Effectiveness	Family
Efficiency	Fascination
Elation	Fashion
Elegance	Fearlessness
Empathy	Ferocity
Encouragement	Fidelity
Endurance	Fierceness
Energy	Financial
Enjoyment	independence
Entertainment	Firmness
Enthusiasm	Fitness
Environmentalism	Flexibility
Ethics	Flow
Euphoria	Fluency

Focus
Fortitude
Frankness
Freedom
Friendliness
Friendship
Frugality
Fun
Gallantry
Generosity
Gentility
Giving
Grace
Gratitude
Gregariousness
Growth
Guidance
Happiness
Harmony
Health
Heart
Helpfulness
Heroism
Holiness
Honesty
Honor
Hopefulness
Hospitality
Humility

Humor
Hygiene
Imagination
Impact
Impartiality
Independence
Individuality
Industry
Influence
Ingenuity
Inquisitiveness
Insightfulness
Inspiration
Integrity
Intellect
Intelligence
Intensity
Intimacy
Intrepidness
Introspection
Introversion
Intuition
Intuitiveness
Inventiveness
Investing
Involvement
Joy
Judiciousness
Justice

Keenness

Kindness

Knowledge

Leadership

Learning

Liberation

Liberty

Lightness

Liveliness

Logic

Longevity

Love

Loyalty

Majesty

Making a difference

Marriage

Mastery

Maturity

Meaning

Meekness

Mellowness

Meticulousness

Mindfulness

Modesty

Motivation

Mysteriousness

Nature

Neatness

Nerve

Non-conformity

Obedience

Open-mindedness

Openness

Optimism

Order

Organization

Originality

Outdoors

Outlandishness

Outrageousness

Partnership

Patience

Passion

Peace

Perceptiveness

Perfection

Perkiness

Perseverance

Persistence

Persuasiveness

Philanthropy

Piety

Playfulness

Pleasantness

Pleasure

Poise

Polish

Popularity

Potency
Power
Practicality
Pragmatism
Precision
Preparedness
Presence
Pride
Privacy
Proactivity
Professionalism
Prosperity
Prudence
Punctuality
Purity
Rationality
Realism
Reason
Reasonableness
Recognition
Recreation
Refinement
Reflection
Relaxation
Reliability
Relief
Religiousness
Reputation
Resilience

Resolution
Resolve
Resourcefulness
Respect
Responsibility
Rest
Restraint
Reverence
Richness
Rigor
Sacredness
Sacrifice
Sagacity
Saintliness
Sanguinity
Satisfaction
Science
Security
Self-control
Selflessness
Self-reliance
Self-respect
Sensitivity
Sensuality
Serenity
Service
Sexiness
Sexuality
Sharing

Shrewdness
Significance
Silence
Silliness
Simplicity
Sincerity
Skillfulness
Solidarity
Solitude
Sophistication
Soundness
Speed
Spirit
Spirituality
Spontaneity
Spunk
Stability
Status
Stealth
Stillness
Strength
Structure
Success
Support
Supremacy
Surprise

Sympathy

Synergy
Teaching
Teamwork
Temperance
Thankfulness
Thoroughness
Thoughtfulness
Thrift
Tidiness
Timeliness
Traditionalism
Tranquility
Transcendence
Trust
Trustworthiness
Truth
Understanding
Unflappability
Uniqueness
Unity
Usefulness
Utility
Valor
Variety
Victory
Vigor
Virtue
Vision
Vitality

The Re-Awakening

Vivacity

Volunteering

Warmheartedness

Warmth

Watchfulness

Wealth

Willfulness

Willingness

Winning

Wisdom

Wittiness

Wonder

Worthiness

Youthfulness

Zeal

Next, we will touch briefly on morals.
Morals are the rules we use to decide if what is good or bad. Each person has their own moral fabric and it is important to define your morals. Morals are the rules that you live by when no one else is looking, how you live your life in private. It is also a good and bad internal scope. Usually morals are set in place by a certain code, dogma, religious sect, spirituality, or a personal internal compass.

In the space below write down the ethics, values, and morals that you were born into, and taught from others, which have influenced your thinking:

The morals + values that I was taught were to be a strong independent woman. Even if you have a man to still handle your business for you + your children. My mother worked hard to take care of us she cherished money and nice things for me + my siblings. So to me love was equated to $. I grew up thinking men should want to take care of their woman. Hand over the money w/no ?'s asked !!

15

Sometimes, as we grow older, or start having our own children, and thinking for ourselves; we decide to employ our own values and morals. These values and morals are different from what we were taught. There are times we have simply outgrown others, or found that what we were taught simply does not serve us any longer.

For instance, early on I was taught that you stick by your man no matter what the circumstance, that as a woman morally you should never leave him if you two are married.

This way of thinking did not serve me and actually, it made me miserable. I ditched the idea that women had to stay in a marriage that they are unhappy in for the sake of children, or because religion said so. I adopted my own morals that a woman should be in a relationship with mutual respect; one where the woman is treated as a gem, with love. I also placed more value on myself, which meant I would not put up with any mistreatment, abuse, or infidelity. I wanted to raise my daughter differently. I want her to become self-sufficient, and to not be afraid to leave a situation, which threatened her self-love, self-esteem, and self-worth.

With the example above, which values, and morals did you ditch once you found it no longer served you? List them here:

1. That I have to always be so strong + independent!

2. That LOVE did not equat to MONEY

3. That men work hard for their $ They should have a say in how funds are spent. Both provide almost equally.

4. That you have multiple kids out ot wet lock instead ot managing your mate.

Emotional Intelligence (EI) is the ability to manage your emotions in a reasonable way in any situation. An emotionally intelligent person is usually a good listener, and no matter what the situation is, they know how to process what is happening in a calm, compassionate, and caring manner without getting bent out of shape. A person who is emotionally intelligent is a person who knows who they are at their very core; they take self-inventory, often tweaking those parts of

17

themselves that are in need of adjustment. This person can look at a problem and rationally, calmly find a solution. Having emotional intelligence also means being aware of how your emotions affect other people around you. Emotional intelligence is the key to success. Emotionally intelligent people usually have the following characteristics in abundance:

1. They Know Themselves: It is actually very important that you know what your values and morals are. What is your driving force in life? In other words, why do you do what you do?

For emotionally intelligent folks, they usually have boundaries set into place, and are very self-aware. They understand their emotions and know how to manage them and keep them under control; no matter the situation. They are constantly taking self-inventory of themselves, and working on those areas that do not serve them well. They understand how they show up in the world.

2. Good Impulse Control: EI people have great impulse control. They do not let a person or situation make them come out of character. They have excellent decision-making skills, and they do not allow others to cross their boundaries. Still they practice this in balance because too little impulse control poses a problem in that the person does whatever comes into mind regardless of the outcome. As well, too much impulse control involves a person never taking risks; and this results in the person becoming rigid, and too restrictive.

3. Empathy: Empathy is the ability to tap into others emotions. Empathetic individuals are great at reading the wants, needs, and desires of others without them having to say too much. To some, this is the definition of intuition. I tend to agree! A person who has empathy has honed their intuitive skills. People who are empathetic are good listeners and are able to relate to others in an exceptional way.

****

Exercise

How do you show up in the world? While it's true you should not to care what others think about you; the people who we allow into our personal space are important to us. Have you taken time out to take inventory to see exactly what they see in you? Let's do this now.

Ask, three people who are closest to you; people who aren't afraid to tell you their truth. You don't want to ask anyone who is too afraid to tell you the truth. These three people can include a family member, spouse, friend, or co-worker. Ask them to write down exactly what they think without fear of repercussions. Again, you want honesty here. Tell them that this exercise will help you take a self-evaluation and that there opinions matter.

1. Do they think you are good listener?
2. Are you an open or closed communicator?
3. Are you a positive, negative or pessimistic person?

Now while they are completing this exercise take the following self-inventory:

Write down who you think you are. Forget about what others think, and society's stereotypes. Who are you, really?

1. Where do you see yourself in 5 years?
2. What are your strengths to make that happen?
3. What are some weaknesses, or obstacles you will face so you can work on them?

After completing the exercises above now answer the following question as best as you can:

Who are you, and what specifically do you want to do next with your life?

CHAPTER 2

OWNING UP TO YESTERDAY: THE KEY TO SHAPING TODAY

"If you don't own your past it will most certainly own you."

As I go down memory lane, I can't help shuddering. My past was certainly tumultuous. It was a never-ending battle of stress, drama, violence, negativity, and letdowns. As a young person, I had no control over it, however I let this lack of control spin me into its web as an adult who always wanted to play the victim card. In actual fact, I was so used to playing victim, and expecting more negativity that when I did experience a little peace it was actually foreign to me.

However, there is one thing to which, ultimately I am grateful to my past for. It has definitely helped in shaping me into the woman I am today.

But how, did I get into this state of freedom from the shackles of my tumultuous past? Walking through life, in an effort to prevent my future from repeating my past, I decided it was time to stop *hiding behind the mask* and do the work.

After facing my past headlong, I learned how it had influenced my life choices. Then I learned how to respect my past, and finally, how to use it as a stepping-stone to launch a brand new life.

Refreshingly, I had been reborn and now, intentionally, I had chosen a new path towards living.

The Power Of Intentional Re-visiting!

One thing I have learnt in this journey- by my experience and that of others is that the past cannot be changed. It has happened and it is written in stone. It is what it is. There is no point wishing it never happened, for wishing cannot undo your past.

However, you can start over and write a new future where you use your past to help you to make informed decisions. Usually, when we bring up our past we tiptoe around it, allude to certain major events that we can remember, or even refuse to bring it up altogether. Heck, most of us suffer from posttraumatic stress disorder (PTSD) or trauma as it normally referred to without even knowing it!

[1]PTSD is a psychiatric disorder that can

occur following the experience or witnessing of life-threatening events such as military combat, natural disasters, terrorist incidents, serious accidents, physical or sexual assault in childhood or adulthood. Given a little time, most of the survivors of trauma return to normal.. Still some survivors will have stress reactions that won't go away on their own, and they need clinical help to cope with these reactions in the form of therapeutic interventions, or even medication. Some will have long lasting effects of the trauma for years to come with what we call PTSD symptoms. For many, these symptoms come in the form of nightmares, flashbacks, and anxiety, with the inability to be in certain surroundings, insomnia, and a feeling of being detached or estranged. An estimated 7.8 percent of Americans will experience PTSD at some point in their lives, with women (10.4%) twice as likely as men (5%) to develop PTSD. About 3.6 % of U.S. adults aged 18 to 54 (5.2 million people) have PTSD during the course of a given year.

People react to trauma in different ways and there are three different sets of symptoms. The first set of symptoms involves re-experiencing or re-living the trauma; much in the way I am asking you to now. If you find yourself becoming irritated, frustrated, upset with the memory (even if you are trying to do something else) you are experiencing

PTSD.

A ready example that comes to my mind is that of a client, whom when I asked to recall the most painful memory of her life, I witnessed her breathing become erratic, after which she reverted to a childlike state, and started to cry uncontrollably. Mind you she was calm, poised, and joyful the moment before I asked her to recall the memory. She had no idea she was reacting in this manner. She did not know that she had PTSD.

The second set of symptoms involves avoidance. Avoidance refers to purposefully staying away from places or people that remind you of the trauma, isolating one's self from other people, or a feeling of numbness.

The third set of symptoms includes things such as feeling on guard, irritable, or getting easily startled.

In this chapter we will purposefully remember certain major life events that either made a profound impact on us, or traumatized us in some way. We are doing this because we *want* to remember, as when we remember we deal with whatever subconsciously still lingers on within our minds, preventing us from being the best we can be.

Believe it or not our brain attempts to protect us from experiencing painful memories by locking them away. You have to understand that in order to overcome trauma it is a good idea to actually confront it and remind yourself, your body, your brain that you are okay, you are safe, and you are finally the one in control. It is a good idea to do some of the exercises in this chapter around a trusted friend or clinician. It is not advised to do this part of the text alone. Bringing up old painful memories can and will trigger us. To trigger means to provoke emotions and memories. Now it's time to revisit those memories to understand what exactly took place, why they happened, and how they affected us.

In the area below, write the most painful memories that had the most profound affect on your life below. I am asking you to dig deep and allow those memories to resurface. It is important that you are in a soothing, and comfortable environment, in other words, in an environment of maximal relaxation. Have a trusted person nearby for support. If any of the memories are too painful to mention; do your best to write them and contact a support person immediately.

Being left allot w/ my older bro + sis + being mistreated because they were young + didnt want that responsibility. My mom pushing me off with gifts rather then embracing my authentic personality

25

Read over what you have just written. How did you feel writing these memories? What physical reaction did you experience by bringing these memories up? How was your breathing? Explain below:

- It helps me release anger + saddness

- The physical reaction I experienced is to want to cry (sad) !!

- My breathing was normal.

Chapter 3

THE ART OF SURRENDERING, ACCEPTANCE AND FORGIVENESS

To Surrender

The dictionary definition of surrender means to cease resisting an enemy or opponent and to submit to their authority[2]. Real freedom comes on the premise of complete surrendering to our past, and putting an end to pretending that events in our past never happened. A horrible past can be seen as our enemy, our opponent and instead of hiding from it we should just submit to it and accept our truth.

To go one step further, we should surrender to God. No, God is *not* our enemy or opponent, yet he is our authority. But, we don't see him as a negative entity that we have to surrender to. We surrender to God's will so that as he takes the driver's seat of our lives, he assumes full control of our lives. With him in control, he can then take our present, and our future and make it significantly better.

When we become 100% honest and truthful about our past, we can respect it. We need to respect it because it helped us become the person we are today.

For instance, I was raised in an abusive environment with domestic violence being the backdrop. Therefore, my father taught me how men ought to, according to him, treat women. I accepted this as truth and set out dating and eventually marrying a man who emulated my father. This type of low self-esteem and low thinking aided me in not seeing myself as God would see me. Therefore, I experienced many negatives because I had blinders on which prevented me from seeing the positive points in my life.

I hid my past and truth for so long because of being scared of what others would say, or losing friends. I hid it because the memories were just too painful. When I finally decided to respect and accept my past I became capable of writing a new chapter in my life. Because I overcame my challenging past, I have become the woman I've always dreamt of being.

Are you able to respect your past? Why or why not?

Yes, because I know my folks were doing the best they could w/ what we had.

What limiting beliefs are currently holding you back? Be 100% honest with yourself.

- Fear of failing
- Not having $
- Confidence is low
- Not enough trust

To Forgive

The concept of forgiveness can really be a hard one to imbibe, for to forgive those who have caused you pain can feel as if you are giving them a free pass to walk all over you as though you're a doormat. It can feel as if you are giving the person, or the situation total control while leaving you helpless and vulnerable. I am here to tell you, that this is not the case at all. To forgive someone that caused you pain, turmoil, or trauma is actually an act of bravery.

It's the one thing that can heal you, and give you total freedom in your mind, body, and soul. When I approached the idea of actually forgiving the people in my life who had caused me trauma, I was apprehensive and actually defiant. I thought to myself, "Why in the world would I, could I, forgive those who purposely put my life in danger, or stomped all over me as if I meant nothing?" Then, a wave of peace came over me, and instinctively I knew that if I didn't forgive them, I would not be able to peacefully move forward.

Dictionary.com defines forgiveness as, to grant pardon for or remission; absolve[3]. I for one don't necessarily believe this definition fits within every scenario. There are simply some acts that are rather hard to pardon. I believe the definition, to cease to feel resentment against is much more aligned with the art of forgiving someone within the context of this forgiveness.

Have you forgiven the acts within your past that you spoke of in the above exercises? Have you forgiven those unspeakable acts that were done against you in your past? Why or why not? Please go to greenlightofforgiveness.com and practice the Green Light of Forgiveness meditation once you answer the above question.

To crown this aspect of forgiveness, I would need to touch on the most important act of forgiveness, which involves forgiving yourself. You must forgive yourself for allowing yourself to have even gone through the turmoil or predicament in the first place. Have you forgiven yourself for your past? Why or why not?

Yes, I had no choice.

@ times I do find my-
self angry ɛ my mother.

31

CHAPTER 4

CHANGE YOUR TAPE: STOPPING THE NEGATIVE MIND CHATTER

"You can't expect to live a positive life if your mind is cluttered with negativity and darkness."

From a logical standpoint, the only things that can be birthed by negative thought patterns are anxiety, depression, and poor self-esteem. Because negative thinking patterns have taken such a strong hold on our lives, we rarely pay attention to them and consequently, have re-wired our brains to accept them as normal thought patterns.

Thus, in the battle against negative thinking, the first step is to pay attention to the exact constituents of our thoughts. Pay attention to those key words that contribute to you feeling bad about yourself.

Let's review the negative things you've told yourself, or the negative things you've replayed in your head all week:

_____

_____

_____

_____

_____

_____

Now answer the following questions concerning the above thoughts:

1. Is there significant proof for the above thought?
2. Is there proof to the contrary of the above thought?
3. Is this a rational thought?
4. What would my friend say if I told them about the situation?

_____

_____

_____

_____

_____

_____

Replace those Negative Thoughts!

"Things do not change, we change." Henry David Thoreau

The first thing I tell my clientele to do when negative thoughts creep into their minds is to police them! To police these thoughts, you have to reserve a portion of your brain that is constantly on patrol for negative thinking 24/7. The police in your brain stop these thoughts from ever forming, and if they do manage to form the police will apprehend and detain these thoughts.

Positive Affirmations

Replace every negative thought with a positive version of those thoughts, so as to combat them. I like to help my clients retrain their brain and to rewire their brains against negative thinking with positive affirmations. Positive affirmations are positive specific statements that help you overcome self-sabotaging, negative thoughts4.

Examples of replacing negative with positive thoughts are:

I'm so fat!	I am currently working on being healthy overall.
I'll never be successful.	I'm currently working hard to achieve my goals to obtain success.
Nothing good ever happens for me!	I'm happy for those who receive blessings; I too will receive the blessings God has in store for me.
I'm so stupid! I always make dumb mistakes.	I'm the bomb! I'm human, and as a human we all make mistakes.

I'm too tired	This is important and I can get this done now.
I am not smart enough	I am smart enough and I can find a solution
I do not know how	I can learn, I can do anything I put my mind to

****

Exercise

Replace each negative thought that you wrote above with a new and improved, positive thought here:

_____

_____

_____

_____

_____

_____

Rubber Band Technique

There is a technique that I learned from a client I mentored who suffered from self-mutilation. Every time she felt the need to cut, she would snap a rubber band on her wrist. I employed this same technique for other clients who had negative self-defeatist habits such as: drug use, cigarette smoking, *OCD (obsessive compulsive disorder)*, anxiety, and negative self-talk.

If you have a judgmental, negative thought pop into your mind, snap your wrist with a rubber band and replace it with a positive thought or affirmation. Then imagine yourself taking that very negative thought, ball it up and toss it way out into the ocean. This imagery helps your mind to physically carry the thought away, banishing it until it is gone for good.

Awareness and Alertness is Key!

Sometimes we are employing negative thinking due to our environment. For instance, I had a client who thought so poorly about herself that it was hard for her to look me in my eyes while we spoke. After some questioning I found out that she surrounded herself with negativity. She watched the most negative television shows that were damaging to women, she listened to music that belittled women, her friends often joked and put her down, and finally she was in a relationship with a man who berated her and emotionally abused her. So with all of this negativity it was easy to see why her own thinking pattern of self was misconstrued, and destructive.

I asked her to go one full week without watching the distasteful television shows and replace them with entertainment that was uplifting and positive. I asked her to refrain from listening to any detrimental or distasteful music. She replaced it with listening to my positive affirmation mp3's, or positive music. She went on to avoid speaking to or seeing her "friends". I never ask a person to leave their significant other; because this is something a person has to do on their own once they have the courage, and strength to do so. I believe that once a person changes their thought pattern and increases their self-esteem they can and will make this decision on their own. She kept a journal and we went over her findings upon our next meeting. She came into that meeting looking well rested, with increased energy, smiled more, and gave me more eye contact. As for the relationship? Well, it took some time, but she is engaged to someone else as we speak!

To know what to change, you have to be aware of what you are changing, and why you should change it. You have to bring your awareness to your own situation and truly confront it. This is the only way you'll truly want to make these changes for yourself.

Energy

"Everything in Life is Vibration" – Albert Einstein

One important step in changing your thinking is being aware of your energy. "If you want to find the secrets of the Universe, think in terms of energy, frequency, and vibration," stated Dr. Nikola Tesla in the year 1942. The whole of the Universe is energy and each basic element of the known atomic chart consists of energy at different rates of vibration. The difference between any two elements is the difference in both atomic structure and vibration rates. There is a frequency or vibration of energy that fills the Universe. This energy is not only beneficial, but also essential to all living cells whether human, plant or animal. Man utilizes this energy with his mind. Every thought is transmitted by this energy. Every aspect of life in the physical depends on this basic energy or power of the Universe[5]. *The law of the universe* states that everything in the Universe moves and vibrates – everything is vibrating at one speed or another. Everything has its own vibrational frequency but we are all connected at the most basic level; *which Professor* John Hagelin calls the unified field[6].

The law of vibration and the law of attraction are parallel to one another. The law of attraction never fails! It only reacts to your vibration. Therefore, if you have a low vibration you will not match with the high vibrational things you are trying to attract. When you align your emotions and feelings with that which you are seeking, you will match the universe and those things will come to you effortlessly.

In terms of money, I had to rewire my way of thinking. While growing up money was an issue for my parents, and I often found my father struggling to make ends meet, or always yearning for abundance but not truly achieving the amount he desired. I did not have good energy where money was concerned, so I either only had enough to make ends meet, I mismanaged it, and thought I didn't deserve it. So when I finally accepted that money is energy, that it is a good tool to do good things, that I deserve it; I started to attract it. In fact, I would attract money without even trying to. It just found its way to me. My vibration and thinking was positive and high about money, and my relationship changed.

With this knowledge, choose each day to match the energy of the universe. It is not possible to be on a high vibration with positive energy every day all day. This is okay. With this new information you will be able to speak positively about yourself, to raise your energy level to match that of the universe.

****

Exercise:

Take a moment to think about your current vibration. On this scale with 10 being the highest vibration and one being the lowest, where are you?

Practice Gratitude

For me, gratitude is a constant action that I practice. I call it an action although it is generally accepted to be a state of being, and this is because I actively practice it. It is something I feel as soon as I wake up, and it is something I express with words directly from my heart.

I am constantly telling the universe how thankful I am for everything that I currently have. I do this because it is important to not only feel the gratitude but express it by minimizing or eradicating complaining, and just feeling thankful every chance you get.

Even in the most destitute situations you can find something to feel thankful for.

America is a first world country and it is true most of us are more fortunate than other citizens of this world who live in third world countries. We have luxury at our disposal, at our fingertips. We have water to drink; in such abundance we can go to a store and purchase it. Some people don't have this. If you start to compare your problems with that of others living in destitute conditions you might feel thankful. I am not trying in any way to minimize your problems, I am just saying try looking for the silver lining, and practicing gratitude. When you practice gratitude for what you do have, and who you are, the universe is ready to give you more. Your energy and vibration increases and you will think a bit more positively about yourself.

****

Exercise

Take out a piece of paper and write down EVERYTHING you are grateful for in the universe. Review this list. Take a deep breath in and upon exhale thank the universe for all that you have.

Mindfulness Meditation

Taking some time out of your busy schedule to just sit and be is essential for resetting your energy. Some people like to sleep while upset or depressed. I find that this can be a dangerous caveat if practiced frequently. Try sitting with your eyes closed for at least 10 minutes a day. Try focusing on your breathing, just *being* conscious of the stream of air that you breath in and out. Don't try and stop your thoughts, allow them to come and then quietly usher *any negative ones* out of your head. This can help you to feel positively about yourself, and it has a positive affect on your physically and emotionally.

CHAPTER 5
WHAT IS YOUR FOCUS?

That you are what you focus on shouldn't come as a surprise. If you want to know your true calling then start jotting down the things you daydream, fantasize, or dream about on a regular basis. What is the one thing that you'd do even if money weren't a factor; the one thing that *d*oesn't feel like work?

For me, I can truly say I absolutely love to encourage and help people. I've been doing it so long that when I started charging for it, it almost felt foreign.

Purpose

Our past can actually be the platform *on* which we build our purpose. *Really, you* didn't go through all of that pain for anything! It's time to turn the lemon into lemonade. In fact you can make it as sweet as you'd like. It can be as simple as a learning experience, or you can make it into a learning experience for others! This is what I've done with my public speaking. It was sweet to have learned from my experiences. However, it was even sweeter to have been vindicated by teaching others how to stay safe, and be compensated along the way. Who doesn't want their pain to turn into glory? Could you use an extra $20k? Of course you could!

We aren't talking Beyoncé here but we want to turn those past lemons into good lemonade. What is the one thing you dream of when you close your eyes? How would you like to earn a living? What do you want to be remembered as? What would you like to be your lemons to lemonade story?

_____

_____

_____

_____

_____

Excuses pacify us but not for long. You know deep within that you are only ignoring your calling by not taking action. Still we need to identify the thoughts that we allow to creep in and hold us back. What are they?

_____

_____

_____

_____

_____

_____

Real Goal Setting

Goals are desired end-points *and while enrolling* in the Pact is not a goal; it's an activity in which the goal should be what you hope to accomplish from this activity (healed from trauma, better self-esteem, gained knowledge of purpose).

SMART goals are goals, which are specific, measurable, attainable, relevant, and time-bound.

Get Specific

We need to be very specific when devising our goals. There is no use having goals that are so broad that they cannot be narrowed down.

For example a goal shouldn't be: I want to someday own my own home. That isn't a specific goal. To make it specific we would say something like, "I want to sell my home within 6 months, and move into a larger home in Collierville, Tennessee which is closer to my office."

Now, this right here is a specific goal, and we could make it even more narrow if we wanted too. With this information in mind, what are your specific goals?

_____

_____

_____

_____

_____

_____

Measurable

Your goals should establish concrete criteria for measuring your progress toward the attainment of each goal you set. For instance if we adopted the above goal we need to make sure we're taking steps The Pact Curriculum to sell our home within 6 months.

Instead of just relying on the realtor to sell our home we will check in with this person, a certain amount of time a week, a day? We would make sure we are measuring our outcomes to ensure our home would sell! Do we need to drop our price? Should we make minor changes to make our home more aesthetically pleasing for a potential buyer?

What things do you need to set into place to make sure your goals are measurable?

_____

_____

_____

_____

_____

_____

Attainable

I love to sing but I know I won't become Beyoncé or Whitney Houston. The same with your goals. They can't be too broad and out of your reach. Along with being measureable they have to be attainable by you or you risk disappointment. How will you ensure your goals are attainable?

_____

_____

_____

_____

_____

Relevant

Your goals have to be relevant to your situation, interests, and skill. If you don't have the necessary skills required to pull off those goals, then make a plan to obtain them.

Are your goals relevant to your life now?

Time-Bound

Well, the thing about things, which do not have an expiry date, is that they cannot be goals!

Your goals have to have an expiration date. Set the timing of your goals so you have the motivation to see them through. The blanket statement, "I want a new bigger home" is much too big and broad. It's like your wishing on a star; the universe will bring it one day, but who knows how far off?

Therefore, pick timeframes within which your goals must have been accomplished. What are your timeframes for completing your goals?

CHAPTER 6

E LAW OF
TION: YOU CAN
AT YOU WANT!

century minds have been
o the Law of Attraction, in the
what have you. In effect, The
has been getting more
d for those of us who actually
proven to be of immense
hievement of a positive and
l business life.

Power of Intention

*Affirmation: I have the strength to accomplish all
that is mine to do.*

Let me intimate you with a truth: You have power. Yes, we all have power- but another truth is that we tap into only a fifth or tenth of it. When we don't recognize the power we hold within, we stifle our growth. When we stifle our growth by not tapping into this strength, we are relying on others to tell us how strong we are.

When you allow others to tell you how strong you are or should be you transfer your power. The universe skips past you when you aren't confident enough to own your own power.

"What we are today comes from our Thoughts of Yesterday, and our present Thoughts build our life of Tomorrow. Our Life is the creation of our Mind." ~Buddha Gautama

The Law of Attraction comes from the idiom, "Like attracts like7." Which generally means the Universe will gift you exactly what you think about. What this means is that whether we realize it or not, we are responsible for bringing both positive and negative influences into our lives.

A key part of the Law of Attraction understands that where you place your focus can have an intense impact on what happens to you. In the prior chapters of The Pact, you "unlearned" how to think. We have retrained your thinking pattern, which is something that has to be constantly put into practice.

How to use the power of intention:

Meditate to calm and clear your mind, visually see what you want to attract, write down what you want to attract, verbalize what you want to attract. Think as if you already have it. Know why you want this "thing" that you are trying to attract.

What exactly do you want to attract from the universe:

_____

_____

_____

_____

_____

Why?

_____

_____

_____

_____

_____

_____

How to Recognize When the Universe is Gifting You

Sometimes the universe is giving us exactly what we ask for but we don't stop to recognize it. We have no idea that it's right in front of us. We have to look for and expect exactly what we were asking for.

If we are so wrapped up in life that we can't slow down to see it, the universe will just keep going. When you are attracting what you want, you will have to look for this blessing. The universe will not give you clues or wake you up to recognize the gift. This is up to you. It's All About Energy

Let's get scientific with quantum physics!

Interestingly, Socrates had said it first when he said that energy, or soul is separate from matter, and that the universe is made of energy. Now science has finally jumped on board confirming that the universe is actually made up of energy and not matter8.

If you want to find the secret of the universe then think in terms of energy, frequency, and vibration. In the past few years here are some examples of what I have been able to attract with a positive mindset, and the law of attraction:

- All expense paid trip to Napa Valley complete with round trip tickets, limousine transportation, green King suite, wine tasting, and 5 star restaurant!
- Representation from a reputable speakers bureau, which resulted in over 20K in extra income.
- TEDx speaker
- Clientele
- Money in personal life and my business life

I used to think I was a magnet for negativity and bad things happening in my life. If something happened that was unpleasant I'd say things like, "I'm not surprised, story of my life!" or even worst, "I should be on a reality show my life has so much drama!" Well the universe brought more of what I stated! I was attracting any and all the drama that happened. So, if you feel as if you just can't get ahead, or that you aren't lucky it's actually because you are attracting just that into your life!

Be Selective: Watch What You Read

With the advent of the Internet we now have so much information at our fingertips, at the drop of a hat. This could be both a good and bad thing. Why? Because just like there is correct and positive information, there is negative information at our disposal. Therefore, you have to put your attention into what you are taking in. Don't just take what you read as the gospel truth, actually take it a step further and research it at the library, ask people who are trained in whatever you are reading, and listen to your intuition.

There are some phenomenal books that I recommend to read if you are searching: Retrain your brain! Written by Bob Proctor; Sleep programming for prosperity; Manifesting Miracles, Esther & Jerry Hicks; Money and the Law of Attraction. These are just a few titles that I like, but then again remember; don't just take my word for it. Research and find out what feels right to you, but keep it positive.

Watch what you view on television because it is programming your brain! Watch only positive programmers because those negative television shows can creep into your mind subconsciously and really do a number on you.

Your music should be positive as well; I like to listen to beautiful music that feels good deep within my soul. Some artists that I find soothing and positive would be Snatam Kaur, Ajeet Kaur, Deva Premal, some Christian, Classical, and Spa music.

My spirit is truly lifted, and I feel the angel's crowd around me when I listen to this serene music.

Watch Your Words:

The universe is set up to gift you, not the other way around. So if you are having thoughts, or take part in conversations like, "It's just me against the world!" or "The world isn't set up for people like me. No matter how hard I try I just can't get ahead." you are pushing the universe out of your thought process and in turn not allowing it to do its real work.

How about words such as, "This is hard!"

Replace such words with, "This is a challenge, but I can handle it." Still if you say words like, "All men are dogs, there aren't any good men left. All men cheat", you will attract men who embody this sentiment.

I hear a lot of my clients proclaim, "There is always something happening to me!" Guess what? You will always have negative events to happen in your life because you are asking the universe to bring negative events into your life. Yeah, that statement actually has a negative undertone to it.

Watch Your Company

The people that you have around you should reflect your positive and high vibrational lifestyle. While it's quite true you can't control others and their action; you can limit the time that you spend in contact with them.

If you have to work with low vibrational energy, zip up before going around them to keep their energy away from you so that it does not affect you.

You might want to ask what zipping means. Zipping is a method whereby you stand shoulder width apart, take in at least three deep meditative breaths, repeat these words, "Archangel Michael I ask that you protect me and my aura away from all negative energy. I ask that you help to keep all my energy in within this boundary, and do not allow it to leave.

Then, from the bottom of you feet pretend that you are zipping in all of your positive energy to the top of your head. When you have totally zipped up state, "And so it is done." You are now zipped! It truly is that easy. So once you have protected your energy you are ready to deal with whatever comes your way. No matter how difficult the person is they cannot have an effect on you.

CHAPTER 7
DECISION MAKING

Decision-making involves choosing a rational choice from the available options. When faced with trying to make a good decision, a person must weigh the positive and negatives of each option, and consider all the alternatives. A visual of what good decision making looks like is in Figure 1 below.

Figure 1. Decision Making Model

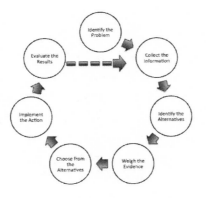

Intuition

Intuition is essentially using your 'gut feeling' to shuffle through potential options. No, God made no mistake when he gifted each of us with intuition. So when you ignore your gut feeling, you are ignoring a very natural part of you that was actually put in place to help you make good decisions. Also, when you ignore your intuition you are essentially saying that you do not trust yourself.

Intuition is a mixture of the things you've gone through in your past and your personal values. It is important to note that it is not always based on reality, leaning more in favor of your perceptions, and if you haven't matured your decisions may reflect that.

This is why it is important to use the decision making model in Figure 1.

I implore you to take your intuition into account. Trust me, I know what could happen first hand when you ignore it. Most of the worst decisions I've ever made in life bordered on ignoring my gut feeling.

No matter how urgent a decision making process seems to you at the time, listen to your gut, and then utilize the decision making model above.

Reasoning

Reasoning is a solid combination of facts and feelings- taking both the facts before you, as well as your intuition into consideration before making a decision. Reasoning effectively has to do with dealing with the present. Be wary of allowing your past experiences to affect the decision that you decide to implement.

When faced with more complicated decisions make sure you use all of the above, howbeit leaving out impulse. Any decision that will result in a long term effect on your life needs to be dealt with carefully considering all those involved as well as the facts, intuition, reasoning, and the decision making model.

Effective Decision-Making

In order for a decision to become effective whether on a personal or professional level you will need to personally stay committed to this decision. You should also be able to help others to see why you arrived at your decision and be able to persuade them to accept this decision. There are some things that can prevent you from making an effective decision and I have discussed some of them below:

1. Information Dearth

Ever walked in the dark, without a torch or light source to guide you along the way? Capture that feeling. This is how not having enough information actually plays out. You are unable to navigate through challenges when there is a dearth of information.

I usually advise my clients to take all the time needed to gather sufficient information before making an obviously informed decision. This way, challenges can easily be sorted out.

2. Too Much Information

Now, this is the direct opposite situation to the above. There is such a thing as too much information!

I've been known to be guilty of gathering too much information and then becoming paralyzed because what is in front of me overwhelms me.

When you have too much information it feels as though you can't see the 'forest for the trees'.

3. Too Many People Involved

Over-involvement of other people in your decision making process is rather burdensome.

Now, you have to consider the values and views of so many other individuals.

Trying to arrive at an effective decision is tough enough on your own, but when you get too many people involved it can get even worst.

So be wary whom you get involved when trying to arrive at a decision, just ensure they know that although, you are open to their suggestions you will come to a final decision on your own.

5. Emotional Attachments

When arriving at the decision make sure it's something you can easily let go. Being too attached to the outcome hampers you from making an effective decision. Surrendering isn't such a terrible notion, seeing as you have put in your very best into the decision making process!

6. No Emotional Attachment

Just as it is not a good thing to be emotionally attached to the decision, it isn't necessarily a good thing when you don't care about the outcome of your decision.

Eventually, an effective decision-making process helps by identifying some very real pros and cons of particular actions, that perhaps you hadn't thought about before.

CHAPTER 8

ESTABLISHING HEALTHY SELF ESTEEM & SELF RESPECT

We all have (or should have) an overall opinion about ourselves, and this is what forms the basis of our decisions and how we process others' opinions of us. A healthy self-esteem stems from an appropriate knowledge of your abilities and limitations.

I like to say that healthy self-esteem involves the positive things you know for sure about yourself. They are the things God loves about you, and which you embrace as well; the positive things that you hold true.

For example I know that I am a compassionate and empathetic individual. I attempt to see the good in everyone first and foremost. I work within my purpose to serve God and God only. I live for honor, truth, and peace. I am the change that I want to see in the world.

Today, I have healthy self-esteem. It wasn't always this way, though.

Looking back, I reflect on those moments in my life when I had hit rock bottom, when the only feeling I had for Toshia was hate. Heck, I couldn't even look at my reflection in the mirror without feeling disgusted. I was utterly repulsed by the entity called me.

But today: well today- I feel blessed to be who and where I am!

If you do not develop healthy self-esteem nor become rooted and strong in who you are as a person, the world will dictate who you are- it will tell you, and remind you every single day of the disgrace that it sees you as.

An unhealthy self-esteem is a strong barrier to becoming whole and healed. You will not be able to operate a heart-centered business with unhealthy, low self-esteem and expect others to become clients, or hire you. If you aren't sure of who you are and exactly what you bring to the table then how will you lead others?

Below write exactly who you are, and not what you think sounds good. Write what God told you about yourself:

Read over what you have just written. Do you believe it within your soul or do you have some reservations? If you have even a small doubt about what you have written, or it was difficult to write fluidly about who you are at your core than you may have unhealthy, and low self-esteem.

I have a simple, yet powerful definition of self-esteem. It is the inability to see yourself as God sees you. If at any time you deny your talents, gifts, perform at a lower level than you ought to, operate on a low vibrational frequency or allow yourself to wallow in the feeling of deserved lack; I have to tell you the truth: there is a problem with your self-esteem.

God did not create you to hide, you must step up to loving yourself, unreservedly and unabashedly;

the way God loves you. This is not operating from the place of Ego, but from a Godly perspective.

You were made in his image, with an anointing to share your gifts with the world: to show others his grace, mercy, and love. If you are not doing this you are operating from a low vibrational place, with low self-esteem.

Limiting Beliefs

Pause for a moment, and think of those beliefs that seemingly hold you back. Their grip on you is so strong that they both literally and figuratively pull you back. Limiting beliefs prevent us from reaching our full potential. They are those pestering thoughts that much like low self-esteem keeps us underperforming. However, unlike low self-esteem they are the false truths that we have heard, seen, or come up with that aren't at all the way God would have us think.

For example, when I had unhealthy low self-esteem I used to think that I wasn't smart enough to become a business owner. I also, thought that success was beyond my reach. I thought it was beyond my reach because I had never seen success before in my family. Some might give me a pass because of ignorance, and shrug my insecurities off as being not my fault, seeing as I'd never really visualized success being attained. This is not an excuse! God told me in my heart that I was supposed to do more, have more, access more. But I allowed what I saw around me, what others thought of me to take over and give me limiting beliefs.

What limiting beliefs are currently holding you back? Be 100% honest with yourself.

_____

_____

_____

_____

_____

_____

Why are you allowing these limiting beliefs to hold you back and keep you playing small?

They Said...

People sure do have a lot to say when it comes to others' lives.

You can see this on social media all day every day. It's a snowball effect. One person can say one thing about something or someone, and then all of a sudden everyone else is saying it! Have you ever discussed something with a friend or relative and all of a sudden they start to give you their unwarranted opinion as if you asked them for it?

What I do know is if you listen to others' opinions you will stay playing it safe, playing small, and you'll be at the mercy of others all the time. For example, once I shared with someone that I had a dream to be an energy healer, or go to school to become a spiritual counselor.

This person began to tell me that I was going to go to hell, and that I had no business wanting to be or do that. That it was against God. I went on for an additional 5 or so years with this yearning going on within me. I started to resent this person for telling me this. I did not pursue it and I felt ill constantly for wanting this so badly.

I allowed this other person's ignorance to hold me back and keep me playing small. Now as a Reiki Master, and spiritual Coach I laugh at how small my thinking was. We cannot give up our gifts, talents, dreams, and goals because others do not understand. The statement, "Quit telling your dreams to people with small minds," holds true. You are to blame if you allow other people to stifle you because they don't get it.

What opinions have people had about you that you allow keeping you on a low vibration?

_____

_____

_____

_____

_____

_____

Here are some ways you can raise your self-esteem and self-respect:

Practice Self-Forgiveness.

If you are carrying around guilt and shame over a past mistake you will find it hard to like or love yourself. You have to understand that humanity comes with a price tag: that of incessant mistakes. The good news is, the more you make these mistakes, and the freer you are to finally climb those heights you ought to climb. No one is perfect therefore; you need to practice compassion of 'self'. Take it easy on yourself, and recognize that we are all flawed. Try the Green Light of Forgiveness meditation that I have on my website, toshiashaw.com. I also go into depth about forgiveness in my book, The Green Light of Forgiveness: A Meditation to Take Over Your Life After Trauma. Once your practice self-forgiveness you will once again be able to take a good look in the mirror and like what you see.

Forget What People Say!

It is good to know where you stand with others, and to know how others view you; but you can't base your self-esteem totally on what others think of you. It is important that you see yourself the way the Creator sees you. You were created, and have a divine purpose. Self-love is key. When you love yourself, you will treat your entire self well inclusive of your soul, mind and body. Also, you won't become an approval addict. Isn't it so sad to watch people who simply live off of others approval? You can see them hanging on to people's every word. Everything they do they are waiting for praise. It's like their saying, "Please like me, please love me, won't you accept me?" These types of people will also seek the approval of others, and be at their mercy.

Watch What You Say About Yourself.

Look everyone has a past, we all have done something we're not proud of, we've all made mistakes, but you can't let these mistakes define you. So don't continue to focus on the mistakes and put yourself down. Whatever you say about yourself you will start to believe. Speak life into yourself by saying encouraging, and positive words.

Seek a Connection With the Divine.

When you have a healthy one-on-one connection with the Creator you will not mentally abuse yourself. You will think of yourself the way the Creator does. You will begin to love and respect yourself unconditionally.

Be Your Own Person.

Healthy self-esteem involves knowing who you are at your core. You will know your morals, and values and not allow anyone to take them from you. It is important that you learn how to stand up for yourself, and be your own person. Don't allow others to boss you around and make decisions for you. Stand firm in who you are.

Keep it Together!

When you allow your emotions to get out of control other people have dominion over you. They will keep pushing your buttons because they know they can get a reaction out of you. So, keep your emotions in check, because being angry and acting out in rage damages a lot of relationships and leads to unhealthy self-esteem and a lack of self-respect.

CHAPTER 9

CREATING BOUNDARIES FOR HEALTHY RELATIONSHIPS

NO Boundaries = Little Self-Esteem

Your boundaries are your values. Boundaries are representative of how much or little you respect yourself. Boundaries are there to help you assert who you are and to teach other people how to treat you.

You have already defined your core values and by now, I really hope that you know who you are. You know what you value. Now you know exactly what you're comfortable with and what you aren't. Once you get clear on what matters most to you, then you can take the bigger step of communicating this to others.

What do you value and what matters to you most in your relationships?

_____

_____

_____

_____

_____

_____

I need to make it clear, at this juncture, that first and foremost, your boundaries are all about you, only you. Instead of creating your boundaries around a specific person or difficult relationship in your life, you must make your boundaries about you. For example, I have set boundaries into place for self-care. It isn't about not specifically taking phone calls on Sunday; it actually borders more on my honoring the fact that I need one day for self-care, rest, and relaxation. This boundary is set in place so that I can decrease my stress level. It isn't about avoiding a particular person's phone calls or distancing myself from loved ones.

Remember, "You are responsible for your quality of life, and overall wellbeing."

You can't expect other people to explicitly know or understand your needs. Yeah, in a perfect

75

world we would be able to change others; but look around- this is no ideal world! Consequently, the only people we can change, in the here and now, is ourselves. However, we can teach people how to treat us. We do this by changing how we deal with them. I am reminded of a suitable quote from Dr. Cloud:

"They may be motivated to change if their old ways no longer work."

When people cross your boundaries decide the consequences well ahead of time.

Now, what do we do if anyone pushes our boundaries (because they will)? Decide what the consequences are. For example, if my boyfriend cheats on me after knowing monogamy is a boundary of mine, I leave the relationship. If a friend of mine calls me on a Sunday after I have shared I would not to be able to talk, I simply do not answer the phone. The best way to figure out your own boundaries and consequences when people cross them is sitting quietly down with yourself and making this all about you. Remember: boundaries are about honoring your needs, not about judging other people's choices.

Let your behavior, not your words, speak for you.

From experience, I have come to the realization that people do not respond directly to what you say. They will however, react to the things that you do. You present your boundaries clearly to people and then let your behavior do the talking. People WILL test, push and disrespect your limits. You'll know you're getting healthier when this doesn't get an emotional reaction out of you. When your boundaries are your core beliefs, you will not get riled up if you are tested.

Say what you mean and mean what you say.

The biggest part of boundaries is HOW clearly you communicate them.

You can have the healthiest set of boundaries on the planet, but if you do not communicate them clearly, you are going to create some really confusing relationships, both for you and everyone else involved.

One way to quickly get someone to question your character or authenticity is to say one thing and do another. For example, if I express to people that I under no circumstances answer my phone on Sunday: but yet I still text back and forth, or even answer their calls then I am being confusing. They will begin to question if this boundary really means anything. They will also question my self-care routine.

Sometimes we're afraid to confront others with truth in love or relationships. We're afraid to tell people what we really want, to admit that we hate going to certain restaurants, or have trouble spending time with a friend's toxic cousin, or hate when a boss dumps deadlines on us at 6pm on a Friday. We conceal our true feelings because we're scared of people's reactions. The more you ground yourself with your boundaries and values, the more you'll be able to be very clear in your communication!

CHAPTER 10
CULTIVATING SELF-CARE
(CHECK UP ON IT, AND CHECK IT OUT)

"Now if you are going to win any battle you have to do one thing. You have to make the mind run the body. Never let the body tell the mind what to do. The body will always give up…"

- George S. Patton

To be a person who is of sound mind, the body must follow. As important as having a sharp, well-rounded mind is, a body, which is, from all points of view, a mess can render the mind inoperable or useless.

It is for this reason I have written this chapter on the cultivation of self-care habits. Together, we will run through a few of your attitudes on health and lifestyle right now.

What are your views as regards the following?

Eating Habits (In the past)

_____

_____

_____

_____

_____

_____

Eating Habits (In the present)

_____

_____

_____

_____

_____

_____

Eating Habits (In the Future)

_____

_____

_____

_____

_____

_____

Physical Fitness (In the Past)

_____

_____

_____

_____

_____

_____

Physical Fitness (In the Present)

_____

_____

_____

_____

_____

_____

Physical Fitness (In the Future)

_____

_____

_____

_____

_____

_____

It might seem a bit stressful and out of place, but it's actually important to know where you stand physically.

We have been dealing with the mental aspects of our lives, but I wouldn't have done justice to this subject matter if I ignore your physical health.

Now the challenge is that most people do either one or the other. They either take very good care of their minds, and neglect their bodies- or vice versa. It's important to take care of the entire package so it can take care of you. In order to live a healthy life we have to take care of all three- mental, physical, and spiritual. When we know our attitudes on physical fitness and food by recognizing, and accepting we will be able to make some positive life choices.

It typically takes 30 days or less to turn a behavior into a habit. The first step is to commit to the challenge. Once you've committed to eating clean for 30 days, your body will follow as your mind directs.

Here are some ways you can make positive changes in your eating habits and physical fitness:

Support. It is very important that you have a good support system. Seek out friends and family who want to see you do well in this area. You don't want the 'know it all,' because they will only piss you off and make you want to quit altogether. It would be better to have someone who can offer an encouraging word, or better yet join you in eating healthy, as well as exercising. Much like you don't want the help of the 'know it all,' you don't want to be the person rubbing it into others faces that you're making positive health changes. It grinds my gears when someone is changing their eating habits and wants their friends or loved ones to do it with them involuntary. I know, it's exhilarating to be finally making so much progress- but remember that this is a personal journey for you; so make it about you, don't push your ideals off on others.

Look in the mirror. Earlier in the workbook I wanted you to start saying nice things to yourself. Now, I want you to do a little mirror work. Go look in the mirror and say, "Hi beautiful! I love you! You deserve the best! You can do it!" By saying nice positive things about yourself, you retrain your brain into thinking this way automatically.

Journaling. Keeping a journal has helped me immensely, and so, I make it mandatory for my clients to journal throughout the mentoring process. Journaling can be a way for you to not only purge your feelings, but to keep up with your progress. Document what you eat, how much you eat, and your physical activity.

Patience. Nothing ever happened in a day. Do not push yourself beyond your limits; you have to give yourself time to heal. Do not rush the process, and be very compassionate towards yourself. Take it easy, and be gentle with you. **Remember, Rome wasn't built in a day!**

Keep Going! Never, ever give up. You might have to take a break when things get too rough, but do not give up. Each day brings along with it, new opportunities. So try again, and keep going. The word 'Quit' shouldn't even be a part of your vocabulary.

30-Day Clean Eating Challenge

Opt for whole, fresh fruits. Fresh fruits and veggies are full of the nutrients and fiber your body needs.

Whole grains. Replace your refined white rice and white bread, both of which have been stripped of their fiber and nutrients, with whole grains such as brown rice and quinoa. Use 5 ingredients or less. Stick to recipes with five ingredients or fewer, and be sure you can pronounce each ingredient. Would you find it on the store shelf? When reading ingredient lists on a package, ask yourself if you would find each ingredient by itself on a store shelf or in your kitchen. If the answer is no, back away.

Meal planning. Taking the time to plan out your meals in advance can prove to be well worth it.

Stay stocked. To ensure that you always have clean, healthy choices available to you, keep your pantry stocked, and a variety of clean eating snacks on hand for when hunger hits.

Fill up on water. Drinking at least four to six glasses of pure water every day will help you stay hydrated.

Eat less, but more frequently. Eat smaller portioned meals, more frequently throughout the day, instead of three large ones.

Eat veggies. Stock up on vegetables to fill your body with nutrients, fiber, and antioxidants.

Dine in. Cooking your own clean meals will not only ensure that you are eating fresh, clean foods, but it will also save you money.

Personally I don't diet, and in my opinion, the word diet is too restrictive. I like to say, I'm making positive life changes regarding my eating habits. This is subconsciously telling my body that we are already making positive changes. Remember, it's important that we retrain our minds.

CHAPTER 11
CONNECTING WITH THE DIVINE

Today, I have received no fewer than 5 mails. In all 5 of them, there is a notable undertone- of emptiness, loneliness, a feeling of disconnect. My response to all of them is similar. Yeah, it is individually crafted- but there is one recurring question in them and it is this question:

'Are you connected to the divine?'

You see the absence of The Divine can leave you feeling unfilled and listless. Years ago before I started practicing spirituality I had those same feelings. It was a gnawing feeling that no matter whom I was around, or what I was doing, I couldn't get rid of the hollow feeling within me.

And I did try to surround myself with those whom I thought mattered. I constantly surrounded myself with people, friends who I felt comfortable with. I went to work in an office surrounded by people, yet I felt alone and miserable. I would go out with friends, yet I felt lonely, unsatisfied, and yearning to be anywhere but where I was.

Now don't get me wrong; a good support structure is absolutely lovely. It's important to have supportive friends and family in your midst. But if in the midst of good company, you still feel alone, you may be missing a divine connection with the creator.

When your crown chakra is open and you have direct communication with your spirit guides, the angels, and the Creator you are never alone. You will find yourself to be in constant company, and at peace. Interestingly, now unlike before, I look forward to time alone. I plan my day around having alone time to connect with my spirit guide, the angels, and the Creator. I do this by meditation, prayer, yoga, and time spent alone in nature.

Connecting

Do not buy into the idea that connecting with the divine is a hard thing, because it isn't.

Some people who are religious may find this easy with prayer. We need to clear a few things up; prayer is you talking to the Divine, while meditating is you listening to The Divine. This is a major difference. Let me explain further here.

While going through my turmoil in my young adulthood, which is basically life, I would fall to my knees often in prayer. I would wail, and moan to God

87

about all of my life's problems. I would ask why I was going through the things that I was experiencing, snot crying, and eyes burning from the tears. Yes afterward I would feel a little better, but after a while the emptiness, and sadness would return. I read the bible as best as I could, I attended church but still felt so alone sitting on the pew with all of the other people in attendance. After church I would drive off of the church parking lot, still searching for answers. That is until I started practicing meditation. I had no idea what I was doing, and back in that day, YouTube wasn't invented, and Google was not as evolved as it is now. So I would have to hightail it to the library to research meditation, which would not have been, a problem except I honestly did not know what I was doing was even called meditation!

I just felt that in order to clear my mind I needed to sit down in one spot, cross my legs and be still. So imagine how inexperienced I was when I first began to do this. All in all, I did just that; and it felt good. So good that I started to do it every day, then I progressed to twice a day, for at least 30 minutes. During my meditation I began to find that my thought process would slow down, until I only had one thought.

And actually, it was a vision. I saw a vision of me, my future self, walking along a beach in a very long, flowy white dress. I would eventually sit down on the beach, and sit and be very still and start to meditate. Imagine that, I meditated that I was meditating! After I was seated in this meditation on the beach, a voice would come into my ear. At first I was alarmed, but after a while I calmed myself and realized that this soothing voice was a soft, and sweet spirit that would speak positively to me. This voice would tell me wonderful things about my life, and myself very lovingly. I began to look forward to this voice every day.

This began my Divine Connection. I felt a new sense of peace that I had never felt before. It made me want to find out more. That more would come in the form of a gentle physical practice named yoga. I found more peace by sitting on a mat, chanting OM, going through a series of poses that made me be in the present. By being in the present I wasn't worried about my future, or feeling anxious as an aftermath of my past.

Later on in life I would find hiking to bring more peace (if that is imaginable) by having me get to ground with the earth, ascending into the mountains with no connection to the hustle and bustle of the city. It was there I found the humor of The Divine. I call God, the great jokester. Amongst nature The Divine has me cracking up with laughter, and filling my heart with love. In nature I pray for humanity, family and friends. I now know that life is more about others and less about me. It is about how I can do my part to spread love and light to a broken world filled with turmoil.

Remain Open

The most important thing to remember when exploring your connection to The Divine is to remain open. Let go of religious dogma, teachings, and preconceived notions. Just open your heart chakra to receiving the sweet gift of light. Remember, The Divine is of light therefore, only allow sweet, soft, encouraging, positive, healing, non judgmental, thoughtfulness into your crown chakra. When we put aside what we think we know about The Divine, The Divine will reveal itself to you without restriction.

Create Your Practice

Whilst making your spiritual practice remember, what works for you, works for YOU. Your spiritual path is unique to you, and no one else. This means it would not benefit you to try and drag others on your spiritual path. This is why most people reject a person who tries to push their religious or spiritual ideals onto them. People respond to how you act, and less to what you say. So be spiritual without being judgmental, and shine your light for others to become attracted to it. Stay within the spirit, and do so without ego.

Make space within your home that is used primarily to practice your spirituality. My bedroom is my sanctuary. I have deities spread around, positive sayings and artwork adorning my walls. I do not have a television in my bedroom because it is distracting. I also have spirituality books and magazines to read. Healing crystals and gemstones sit upon my altar. Live plants sit in the windowsill to give oxygen and to beautify my space. My yoga mats line up against the wall, so that I can quickly grab them to stretch in the morning and evening. This is just an example of how to have sacred space to practice your spirituality to connect with The Divine.

Your connection to The Divine will bring harmony and guidance from your spirit guides, the angels, and will define your life and bring you purpose. If you want to find your Pact, if you want to get re-awakened, you've got to find your connection with the Divine.

CHAPTER 12
FORGET FEAR

Fear is an illusion it is not real. Fear is your body's flight or fight response to the unknown. Many of us know this to be true theoretically, but not practically. Although, it is a natural emotion, it should not settle into your body and be allowed to take up space there. If you allow fear to take up space it will make stems within your root chakra and begin growing. It will spread throughout your chakras, eventually making its way up to your crown chakra where you will no longer be able to hear The Divine. It creates health problems and can stagnate you until you can no longer operate without it.

"Fear stifles our thinking and actions. It creates indecisiveness that results in stagnation. I have known talented people who procrastinate indefinitely rather than risk failure. Lost opportunities cause erosion of confidence, and the downward spiral begins."
~ Charles Stanley

You started out reading The Re-Awakening with fear of the unknown. Now that you have learnt that leaving the past behind you is no impossibility that you can now move towards a profitable and brighter future your fear should have dissipated. Still, you might carry on concern for what your future looks like beyond, The Awakening. Let us acknowledge and dissect the fear that arises now.

I am fearful of the following:

_____

_____

_____

_____

_____

_____

Now let's review, are your fears valid, or are they illusory? Let's go over facts as opposed to what your brain is making up for you.

Just Breathe

As I slowly inhale, I breathe in trust, and slowly exhale fear. I breathe in trust, and bring it down into the bottom of my stomach and then all the way down to my toes. As I exhale fear, I expel it from my mind and lungs.

Meditation to Banish Fear

I continue to do this simple meditation exercise until I can feel the energy shift within and around me. I draw in light to myself as I focus on and renew my trust in my higher power.

After I am centered, I move into my day with positive energy and a knowing that everything is going to be all right. If I feel myself start to slip back into those mopey feelings, I begin to breathe in trust all over again, until the feeling subsides.

12 Ways to Overcome Fear Right Now:

Recognize. Before you can overcome something you have to recognize that you have it. If you don't recognize your fear and become aware of it you will overlook it and it will grow. Get 100% honest with yourself and recognize what you are fearful of by writing it down (just like you have done earlier within the text), and where it is coming from. Remember, that you are not your fear. Your fear is an illusion and not at all you.

Accept. Accept that you have this fear. One reason people keep being fearful of things is because they pretend that they're not. They deny, deny, deny.

This denial only keeps them connected to the fear, and in their mind it makes the fear real. Just accept that you have the fear. Your admission will help you acknowledge it and be able to face it head on.

Get Curious. Start to examine just why you have this fear, where did it come from anyway? Is this something that you became fearful of on your own, or was it given to you? For example a client of mine was fearful of success. No matter that she had already achieved what most people would consider success (college graduate, landed a wonderful career) she just couldn't accept that she had it and was scared of not achieving what she thought looked like success in her life. Well, after working with me one on one in The Re-Awakening, she realized that her parents gave this fear of failure to her. Her parents would treat her as if she weren't good enough, smart enough and therefore, wouldn't amount to much. She had to realize that the fear wasn't her fear at all. So, become curious as to just where the fear culminates from; did you come up with it on your own, or was it given, or simply passed on to you?

Surrender. Ever heard the expression, let go and let God? Well, it's true! If you surrender or give up your need to control things and let The Divine handle your life's load you will be much better off. It's not easy giving up our need to control things, but how has that worked out for you so far? It's far better to just throw your hands up and allow Spirit to guide you.

Emotional Freedom Technique or Tapping (EFT). Tapping is a wonderful way to tackle fear head on. Use your fingers to tap on various points of your body while stating positive affirmations. I use tapping in my own life whenever I am faced with stress, and on my clients to help relieve trauma symptoms. I take two fingers and very lightly tap on: top of the head, middle of forehead, sides of temples, underneath the eyes, underneath the nose, underneath the mouth, on the collar bones, in the middle of chest, and side of hand. I repeat the affirmation, "Even though I am fearful of (state what you are afraid of), I lovingly accept and appreciate myself." Just repeat this mantra after every pressure point. It's amazing, how much it works!

Gratitude. I would have to say that gratitude is at the center of my life. I practice it every morning and evening. If you are constantly grateful for your life and for all that you have, it makes it difficult to focus on what's wrong, what you don't have, and the fear that arises from this.

Journaling. Journaling is essential in getting your fears down on paper so that you can actually read them and gain an understanding of where they are coming from. When you think of your fears you are only going on an endless loop of misery. But while journaling, you can finally free yourself of those dampening thoughts without actually 'thinking' them.

Read. Read positive books, and print magazines to keep you empowered. Read things that will give you hope, not push you further towards your fear. Only internalize positive print.

Pray. When we pray to The Divine we are giving it to him and walking away. You don't have to keep the fear. Give it to your God in prayer. Have faith in what you believe in.

Physical Activity. Get physical and exert all that bad energy. Don't allow negativity to become trapped in the body. Work out, or do yoga.

Get Help. Getting the help of a therapeutic clinician or life coach can work wonders on dissipating fears. They can listen to your fears, and help you work through them.

Watch What You Eat. Try eating clean, cut down on sugar, additives, and processed foods. When you eat clean, coupled with exercise, you can think clearer. You also become more positive overall.

I have a simple regimen, which I'd implore you to follow:

Try the above mentioned things for at least 10 days, and journal your outcome. If you like the outcome, then try to continue 10 more days. Increase the amount of days until you lose count and it becomes a new way of life for you. You will be

surprised at how your fear will leave your
subconscious mind.

CHAPTER 13
THE IMPORTANCE OF AUTHENTICITY & LIVING IN YOUR TRUTH

To live your pact, after being re-awakened; it is important for you to live your truth. Early on in this workbook you identified your morals and values. Overtime those values and morals have changed, if you are in doubt about this. Go back to the beginning and once more identify your values and morals; have they changed? I would guess that they have. Why? Because as you let go of your past, and start opening up to your truth you start to identify who you truly are. While doing this your values and morals undergo transformation. When you start to live in alignment with what matters to you most, you begin to live in your authenticity, by living your truth.

You Will Find Freedom by Living Your Truth

I remember the burden of hiding behind the truth of who I was and what I'd been through. I lived for years with the pain of my past choking my throat chakra like a tightly worn cloak. It wasn't until decided to become authentic by confronting my past, getting over my trauma, and defining what mattered the most to me that my life truly began to blossom.

You'll Be Better Prepared for the Throws of Life

When you are open and honest with yourself, the burden of hiding your past is gone. Having a strong sense of self enhances your resilience, provides you with an anchor and enables you to face challenges with a more balanced outlook, confident that regardless of what happens, you will be okay.

You Won't Need the Validation of Others

Living your truth means that you form a new relationship with yourself. This new relationship with self will be based on the foundation that you know who you are as a person. There will be no need to seek external validation. When you look to others to define who you are and to approve of who you are it becomes disempowering. You will hand over your power when you need them to reassure you that you measure up, that you're enough, that you fit in. Fit into what? You are who you are, and who you are is enough. It's okay to have friendly support, but the problem lies within needing this external support to live your life. Look to yourself for strength, approve of yourself. Once you do this you will attract those who respect you for being your true self.

Use Your Voice

The most challenging part of living your truth would be standing up, with eyes lifted and using your voice to speak your truth. But the truth is, once you recognize, accept, and surrender to the Spirit, you will be able to use your voice. You will also be able to speak up on behalf of yourself. Things that you used to allow to slide and happen to you will no longer happen because you will be able to self-parent yourself and speak up.

Screw Guilt!

When you are standing in your truth you will have the foundation to stand up for yourself, make solid decisions, establish and maintain healthy boundaries. You will look to self first and foremost, and you will have a clear mind to take care of yourself, and establish healthy self-care

You will use your values to know who you are at your core and determine what you stand for. You will also know your strengths and weaknesses, and strive to have healthy self-talk. You will do more of what makes you happy.

How will you begin to live your truth?

_____
_____
_____
_____
_____
_____
_____
_____
_____
_____

CHAPTER 14
MOVING FORWARD:
WHERE DO YOU GO FROM HERE?

Embracing Your Freedom

When you live your truth, learn how to respect your past, compassionately accept who you are, and where you are in the present you will find yourself living freely. In order to embrace your freedom you will need to use your new goals to cultivate your pact, to ensure that you are re-awakened. You will have to embrace courage to stay on track to deliver on that promise to yourself. In doing so you will be able to find your voice, and use it without apology.

It is time to embrace your new normal, your new way of living. Ease into this new feeling of freedom. Refrain from looking back, or over your shoulder in search of the old you, or your old life. It's gone and you've done the work.

Remember the three steps, Recognize, Accept, and Surrender all to the universe. Embrace your newfound freedom, and embrace the new you.

About the Author

Toshia Shaw is a Human Services professional who specializes in behavioral health, holistic mental health, and energy healing. She mentors women who suffer from the effects of drug addiction, sexual assault, human trafficking, domestic violence, grief, loss, and other traumatic experiences, which shape the way they view themselves and the world around them. She is the Founder and Executive Director of Purple W.I.N.G.S. (PWs), a 501 c (3) non-profit all girls mentoring organization; and Toshia Shaw, The Professional Mentor, LLC, is a trauma-informed, life coaching agency, and energy healing company.

She is an accomplished, motivational speaker who routinely travels the country to share her message. As a life coach, she helps women who have experienced traumatic events in their lives to overcome their past traumas and transform their lives. Through workshops, group mentoring, e-courses, and one-on-one coaching, Toshia helps others to cultivate a new way of living that will enable them to attract the kind of relationships, success, and happiness that they truly deserve.

Toshia is a certified Reiki Master, and intuitive healer combining spirituality and intuition, with the use of the five senses to locate and correct imbalances in the energy flow within the body. She does this by touch and long distance healing where she focuses on physical, emotional, and sexual wellness.

To get in touch with Toshia, simply visit her website, ToshiaShaw.com.

References

Nebraska Department of Veterans' Affairs (2007). Retrieved on January 2015 from http://www.ptsd.ne.gov/what-is-ptsd.html.

* English Oxford Living Dictionaries (2017). Retrieve on January 2017 from https://en.oxforddictionaries.com/definition/us/surrender.

* Shaw, T. (2016). "The Green Light of Forgiveness: A meditation on forgiveness to take total control over your life after trauma." Purple Wings Publishing.

* Mindtools: Essential Skills for an excellent career (2017). Retrieved on January 2017 from https://www.mindtools.com/pages/article/affirmations.htm.

* Reflection Magazine (1998). The Universal Energy of Vibrations, Issue No. 9. Retrieved on December 2016 from https://www.bibliotecapleyades.net/ciencia/esp_ciencia_universalenergy01.htm.

* The Law of Vibration (2009-2016). One Mind – One Energy: The Power is Within. http://www.one-mind-one-energy.com/Law-of-vibration.html